LEBANESE

COOKBOOK

40 Easy Recipes For Traditional Food From Lebanon

Adele Tyler

SUMMARY

Chapter 5: Modern recipes

Lebanese Grilled Eggplant with Yogurt Sauce
Lebanese-Style Quinoa Salad
Kibbeh Nayyeh (Raw Kibbeh)
Lebanese Roasted Vegetable Pita Sandwiches
Lebanese Rice Pudding with Rose Water

Chapter 6: Desserts

Qatayef
Znoud El Sit
Ghraybeh
Layali Lubnan
Cheese Knefeh
Honey Ashta

Chapter 7: Drinks

Sahlab (hot milk and spices drink)
Sweet Lime Drink (Assir Limoun)
Orange Blossom Water (Ma Zahar)
Grape Syrup Drink (Sharab Al-inek)
Lebanese Iced Tea (Shai Baida)

Conclusions

INTRODUCTION

Lebanese cuisine is a celebration of the country's rich cultural heritage, history, and its diverse blend of flavors, textures, and cooking styles. From the Mediterranean coast to the mountains, Lebanese cuisine is a fusion of regional dishes that reflect the diverse cultural influences of the country's history. From hearty stews and tangy pickles to delicate sweets and refreshing drinks, there is something for everyone in Lebanese cuisine.

Lebanese cuisine is renowned for its emphasis on fresh ingredients and bold spices, and its use of herbs, such as mint, parsley, and basil, is what sets it apart from other cuisines. The Lebanese have always placed great importance on hospitality, and the preparation of good food is a key part of this tradition. Meals are often served in large quantities to be shared with family and friends, and the art of cooking is passed down from generation to generation. The Lebanese diet is largely based on vegetables, grains, legumes, and meats, making it not only delicious but also healthy.

One of the defining features of Lebanese cuisine is its mezze, a collection of small dishes that are served before a meal. This allows for a variety of flavors and textures to be enjoyed before the main course. Mezze can include anything from dips and spreads to salads, grilled meats, and vegetables, and some of the most popular mezze dishes include hummus, baba ganoush, and tabbouleh. Another hallmark of Lebanese cuisine is its use of flatbreads, such as pita, to scoop up dips, fill with meats or vegetables, or wrap around ingredients. Flatbreads are a staple in Lebanese cooking and are used in a variety of dishes.

In this Lebanese cuisine cookbook, you will find a collection of authentic and traditional recipes that have been passed down through families and passed on to new generations. Each recipe is accompanied by a detailed explanation of ingredients, cooking techniques, and the history of the dish. Whether you are experienced cook or a beginner, this book will guide you through the steps to create delicious and authentic Lebanese dishes in your own kitchen.

From traditional stews and casseroles to grilled meats and vegetables to sweet treats and refreshing drinks, you'll find recipes for a wide range of dishes in this cookbook. Some of the must-try dishes include Kibbeh Nayeh, a raw lamb dish that is blended with bulgur, onions, and spices; Tabbouleh, a refreshing herb salad made with parsley, mint, and bulgur; and Mujadara, a hearty lentil and rice dish seasoned with spices and caramelized onions.

Lebanese cuisine is also renowned for its sweet treats, and this cookbook includes recipes for traditional sweets such as Baklava, a flaky pastry made with phyllo dough and sweetened with honey and nuts; and Nammoura, a semolina cake flavored with orange blossom water and topped with a sweet syrup. You'll also find recipes for refreshing drinks like Arak, a clear anise-flavored liquor, and Sharbat, a sweet syrup made from fruit and flower extracts that is mixed with water to create a refreshing beverage.

In conclusion, Lebanese cuisine is a celebration of the country's rich cultural heritage and its diverse blend of flavors, textures, and cooking styles. This cookbook is a guide to preparing delicious and authentic Lebanese dishes in your own kitchen, with recipes that cater to both seasoned and novice cooks. Whether you're looking to host a dinner party or just want to enjoy a home-cooked meal, this cookbook has everything you need to bring the flavors of Lebanon to your kitchen.

CHAPTER 1

Appetizers

Lebanese cuisine is celebrated for its diverse and flavorful dishes, and the appetizers, or mezze, play a crucial role in enhancing the dining experience. The mezze platter, a collection of small plates meant to be shared amongst diners, is a staple of Lebanese dining, offering a range of flavors, textures, and aromas to stimulate the senses. This diverse array of dishes is not just an appetizer, but a window into the rich culinary heritage of Lebanon.

Mezze is a unique and memorable dining experience, showcasing the versatility and creativity of Lebanese cuisine. Each dish is carefully crafted to offer a harmonious blend of flavors and ingredients, from tangy dips like hummus and baba ganoush to crunchy and fragrant salads like fattoush and tabbouleh, to bite-sized morsels like kibbeh and falafel. Aromatic herbs like mint, parsley, and cumin add depth and complexity to the flavors.

Lebanese cuisine prioritizes the use of fresh, seasonal ingredients, and this is especially true for mezze dishes. From juicy summer tomatoes to crisp cucumbers, the ingredients are chosen for their quality and taste and often sourced from local markets. This focus on fresh ingredients, combined with the use of spices and herbs, makes Lebanese mezze not only delicious but also nutritious.

The presentation of a mezze platter is a visual feast, with each component carefully arranged to create a stunning display. The platter is often served with freshly baked pita bread, which acts as the perfect vessel for scooping up dips or wrapping around fillings.

This book brings the authentic flavors and techniques of Lebanese cuisine to your kitchen, with a collection of delicious and easy-to-follow mezze recipes.

Did you know that...

1. Lebanese cuisine has been influenced by various civilizations including the Phoenicians, Arabs, and Ottoman Turks.
2. The tradition of serving a variety of small dishes, known as mezze, dates back to ancient times in the Middle East.
3. Hummus, a creamy dip made from chickpeas, is said to have originated in Egypt but became popular in Lebanon and the surrounding region.
4. Tabbouleh, a salad made from parsley, mint, bulgur wheat, and other ingredients, is a staple of Lebanese cuisine and is often served as part of a mezze platter.
5. Baba ghanoush, a dip made from eggplant, tahini, and spices, has been enjoyed in the region for hundreds of years.
6. Kibbeh, a dish made from ground meat and bulgur wheat, is considered a national dish of Lebanon and is often served as an appetizer.
7. Falafel, deep-fried balls made from chickpeas, is a popular street food in Lebanon and can be found in many mezze platters.
8. Stuffed grape leaves, known as warak enab, are a common appetizer in Lebanese cuisine and are typically filled with rice, herbs, and spices.
9. Fattoush, a refreshing salad made with pita bread and a variety of vegetables, is a staple of Lebanese cuisine and is often served as an appetizer or side dish.
10. Lebanese cuisine has a long history of incorporating herbs and spices, including mint, parsley, sumac, and allspice, to add flavor to dishes.

Falafel

This classic falafel recipe is a staple of Lebanese cuisine and is enjoyed by people all over the world. Falafel is a deep-fried ball made from chickpeas, spices, and herbs, and is typically served in a pita bread with toppings such as tahini sauce and salad. The dish is believed to have originated in Egypt, but it has since become popular throughout the Middle East and beyond.

 4 SERVINGS   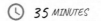 35 MINUTES   150 KCAL    EASY

INGREDIENTS

- 1 cup dried chickpeas
- 1 onion, chopped
- 3 cloves garlic, minced
- 1/2 cup parsley, chopped
- 1/2 cup cilantro, chopped
- 2 tsp. cumin
- 1 tsp. coriander
- 1 tsp. baking powder
- 1/2 tsp. salt
- 3 tbsp. all-purpose flour
- Oil for frying

DIRECTIONS

1. Before you begin, make sure you have soaked your chickpeas in water overnight or for at least 8 hours. This will help soften the chickpeas, making them easier to process and resulting in a smoother, more delicious final product.
2. Once the chickpeas have soaked, it's time to start making your falafel mixture. Start by draining the chickpeas and adding them to a food processor along with the onion, garlic, parsley, cilantro, cumin, coriander, baking powder, and salt.
3. Pulse the ingredients in the food processor until they are well combined and have formed a thick paste. The mixture should be dense and hold together, but still have some texture to it. If the mixture is too thin, add a little more flour to help thicken it up.
4. Once the mixture is ready, it's time to form your falafel balls. Using your hands, take a spoonful of the mixture and form it into a ball. Repeat this process until you have used up all the mixture and have formed around 8 balls.
5. Now it's time to fry your falafel! Heat oil in a deep pan until it reaches 375°F. You can use a thermometer to ensure that the oil is at the correct temperature, or you can test it by adding a small piece of the falafel mixture to the oil. If it sizzles and starts to brown immediately, the oil is hot enough.
6. Carefully place the falafel balls in the hot oil, making sure not to overcrowd the pan. Fry the balls for 3-4 minutes or until they are golden brown and crispy. Use a slotted spoon to remove the falafel from the oil and place them on a paper towel to remove any excess oil.
7. Your falafel is now ready to be served! Place a few balls in a pita bread and add any toppings you like, such as tahini sauce and a fresh salad. The combination of the crispy falafel balls and the creamy tahini sauce is truly a match made in heaven!

Baba Ghanoush

Baba Ghanoush is a popular Middle Eastern dip made with eggplant, tahini, olive oil, lemon juice, and seasonings. It is a staple in Lebanese cuisine and is typically served with pita bread or vegetables.

 4 SERVINGS   20 MINUTES   100 KCAL   EASY

INGREDIENTS

- 1 large eggplant
- 2 tablespoons tahini
- 2 tablespoons olive oil
- 1 clove garlic, minced
- 2 tablespoons lemon juice
- 1/2 teaspoon salt
- 1/4 teaspoon ground cumin
- 2 tablespoons parsley, chopped (optional)

DIRECTIONS

1. Start by preheating your oven to a toasty 400°F (200°C). This is an important step as the high heat will help to caramelize the eggplant, giving it that delicious smoky flavor that Baba Ghanoush is known for.
2. Once the oven is ready, take a large eggplant and give it a few gentle pokes all over with a fork. This will allow steam to escape as the eggplant roasts, preventing it from exploding in the oven.
3. Place the eggplant on a baking sheet and pop it into the oven. Roast for 20-25 minutes, or until the skin is blackened and the eggplant is soft and tender to the touch.
4. When the eggplant is done roasting, take it out of the oven and let it cool for a few minutes. The skin should peel away easily, revealing the soft, creamy flesh inside.
5. Once the eggplant has cooled, transfer it to a food processor along with 2 tablespoons of tahini, 2 tablespoons of olive oil, 1 minced clove of garlic, 2 tablespoons of lemon juice, 1/2 teaspoon of salt, and 1/4 teaspoon of ground cumin.
6. Blend everything together until you have a smooth, creamy mixture. If the mixture is too thick, add a splash of water to thin it out.
7. Transfer the Baba Ghanoush to a serving bowl and sprinkle with 2 tablespoons of chopped parsley (if using).
8. Serve the Baba Ghanoush with warm pita bread or fresh vegetables. Dip, savor, and enjoy! The smoky, tangy, and creamy flavors will dance on your taste buds and leave you wanting more.

Grilled Halloumi Cheese

Halloumi cheese is a staple in Lebanese cuisine, known for its firm texture and salty, tangy flavor. The cheese originated in Cyprus, but has since become popular throughout the Middle East and Mediterranean, particularly in Lebanon.

 4 SERVINGS   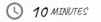 10 MINUTES   200 KCAL    EASY

INGREDIENTS

- 8 ounces of Halloumi cheese, sliced 1/2 inch thick
- 2 tablespoons olive oil
- Salt and pepper to taste
- Fresh herbs, such as mint or parsley, for garnish (optional)

DIRECTIONS

1. Slice the Halloumi cheese into 1/2 inch thick pieces.
2. In a small bowl, mix together the olive oil, salt, and pepper.
3. Place the cheese slices in a single layer in a large dish, and brush both sides of each slice with the olive oil mixture.
4. Preheat a grill or grill pan over medium-high heat.
5. Once the grill is hot, place the cheese slices on the grates. Cook for 2-3 minutes on each side, or until the cheese is golden brown and slightly charred.
6. Remove the cheese from the grill and place on a serving platter.
7. If desired, sprinkle with fresh herbs and additional salt and pepper to taste.
8. Serve immediately, while the cheese is still hot and melted.

This dish is best enjoyed on its own, or as a tasty addition to a Mediterranean-style salad. It can also be served as a flavorful appetizer, perfect for sharing with friends and family. The tangy, salty flavor of the Halloumi cheese is a delicious contrast to the crisp, juicy flavors of fresh vegetables, making it a versatile and flavorful dish that is sure to please. So why wait? Light up your grill and get ready to enjoy this classic Lebanese treat!

Arnabit

Fried Cauliflower, also known as Arnabit, is a traditional Lebanese dish that is both flavorful and easy to prepare. The dish is made by coating florets of cauliflower in a batter made from seasoned flour and frying them until they are golden and crispy.

 4 SERVINGS    **30** MINUTES   **200** KCAL    EASY

INGREDIENTS

- 1 large head of cauliflower, cut into florets
- 1 cup all-purpose flour
- 1 teaspoon salt
- 1 teaspoon paprika
- 1/2 teaspoon black pepper
- 1/2 teaspoon garlic powder
- 1/2 teaspoon onion powder
- 1/2 teaspoon cumin
- 1/4 teaspoon cayenne pepper
- 1 cup water
- Vegetable oil for frying

DIRECTIONS

1. Rinse the cauliflower florets and pat them dry.
2. In a large mixing bowl, whisk together the flour, salt, paprika, black pepper, garlic powder, onion powder, cumin, and cayenne pepper.
3. Slowly add in the water while whisking, until the batter is smooth and has a thick, but pourable consistency.
4. In a large, heavy-bottomed pot, heat the vegetable oil over medium-high heat until it reaches 375°F.
5. Dip the cauliflower florets in the batter, one at a time, using tongs or your hands, shaking off any excess.
6. Carefully place the battered cauliflower into the hot oil, working in batches to avoid overcrowding the pot. Fry for 3-4·minutes, or until the florets are golden brown and crispy.
7. Remove the fried cauliflower from the oil with a slotted spoon, and place on a paper-towel lined plate to drain excess oil.
8. Serve immediately, while the cauliflower is still hot and crispy, with a sprinkle of additional salt if desired.

Fried Cauliflower is a delicious and flavorful dish that is perfect for serving as an appetizer or as a side dish with a main meal. The crispy exterior and tender interior of the cauliflower make it a satisfying and satisfying treat. The addition of spices and seasonings gives the dish a bold and flavorful profile that is sure to please. So, what are you waiting for? Get cooking and experience the delicious taste of traditional Lebanese cuisine!

Soujouk

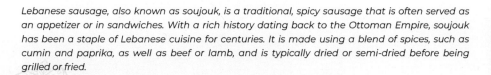

Lebanese sausage, also known as soujouk, is a traditional, spicy sausage that is often served as an appetizer or in sandwiches. With a rich history dating back to the Ottoman Empire, soujouk has been a staple of Lebanese cuisine for centuries. It is made using a blend of spices, such as cumin and paprika, as well as beef or lamb, and is typically dried or semi-dried before being grilled or fried.

 4 SERVINGS   2 HOURS   200 KCAL    MED

INGREDIENTS

- 1 lb beef or lamb, minced
- 1 tsp ground cumin
- 1 tsp paprika
- 1 tsp dried red pepper flakes
- 1 tsp salt
- 1 tsp dried thyme
- 1 tsp ground coriander
- 1 tsp garlic powder
- 1 tsp black pepper
- 1 tbsp tomato paste
- 1 tbsp olive oil
- 1 tbsp lemon juice
- Natural sausage casings or aluminum foil

DIRECTIONS

1. In a large mixing bowl, combine the minced meat, cumin, paprika, red pepper flakes, salt, thyme, coriander, garlic powder, black pepper, tomato paste, olive oil, and lemon juice. Mix well using your hands to ensure all ingredients are fully incorporated.
2. Marinate the sausage mixture in the refrigerator for at least 2 hours, or overnight for the best flavor.
3. After marination, stuff the mixture into sausage casings or form into sausage shapes using aluminum foil.
4. Heat a grill or griddle over medium-high heat. Place the sausages on the grill and cook for 10-12 minutes, turning occasionally, until fully cooked.
5. Serve the soujouk hot with pita bread or your favorite dipping sauce.

Lebanese sausage is a delicious and flavorful dish that is perfect for those who enjoy spicy food. Its unique blend of spices, along with the tender and juicy meat, makes for a savory and satisfying experience. Whether you are looking for a spicy appetizer or a delicious sandwich filling, soujouk is the perfect choice. So, grab some friends, fire up the grill, and enjoy the authentic flavors of Lebanese cuisine with this classic dish.

Batenjan

This classic Lebanese dish, Fried Eggplant (Batenjan), is a staple of Lebanese cuisine and a staple at mezze platters across the country. It is a simple, yet delicious dish that is made by frying slices of eggplant and then seasoning them with a combination of spices, garlic, and lemon juice.

 4 SERVINGS   30 MINUTES   150 KCAL   EASY

INGREDIENTS

- 2 medium eggplants, sliced into rounds
- 1 cup all-purpose flour
- 2 eggs, beaten
- 1 cup breadcrumbs
- Salt and pepper, to taste
- 2 cloves of garlic, minced
- 2 tbsp. lemon juice
- 2 tbsp. chopped parsley
- Vegetable oil for frying

DIRECTIONS

1. In a large bowl, combine the flour, salt, black pepper, paprika, and dried thyme.
2. Dip each eggplant slice into the flour mixture, making sure to coat both sides evenly.
3. In a large skillet, heat the vegetable oil over medium heat.
4. Fry the eggplant slices in the hot oil until they are golden brown on both sides, about 2-3 minutes per side.
5. Remove the eggplant slices from the oil and place them on a paper towel-lined plate to drain excess oil.
6. Serve the fried eggplant hot with your favorite dips and sauces.

Enjoy your delicious and traditional Lebanese dish of Fried Eggplant (Batenjan)! The crispy exterior and soft interior make for a satisfying bite, and the seasoning adds a burst of flavor in every bite. Pair it with hummus, tahini, or garlic sauce for a delicious meal.

CHAPTER 2

Soups and Salads

Soups and salads are a staple in Lebanese cuisine, offering a range of flavors and ingredients that reflect the diverse culture and geography of the country. The warm, sunny Mediterranean climate of Lebanon provides an abundance of fresh produce, making salads a staple on any Lebanese table. From the simple chopped vegetable salads, like fattoush, to the more complex, protein-packed tabbouleh, salads are a healthy and flavorful way to start a meal.

Soups, on the other hand, are an essential comfort food in Lebanese cuisine, offering warmth and sustenance during the cooler months. From the traditional lentil soup, or "ads," to the hearty vegetable soup, or "shorbet," soups in Lebanese cuisine are typically filled with hearty ingredients such as beans, lentils, and vegetables, making them both filling and nutritious.

In this chapter, we will explore the world of Lebanese soups and salads, showcasing the diverse ingredients, spices, and cooking methods used in these traditional dishes. We will also provide step-by-step instructions and tips to help you create restaurant-quality soups and salads in the comfort of your own kitchen. Whether you're looking for a light and refreshing lunch, or a warm and comforting dinner, the recipes in this chapter are sure to delight.

Lebanese soups and salads are not only delicious, but they are also an essential part of a healthy diet. They are packed with fresh vegetables, herbs, and spices, providing essential vitamins, minerals, and antioxidants. They are also low in calories, making them a great option for those who are watching their weight.

In this chapter, we will showcase the most popular soups and salads in Lebanese cuisine, each with its unique flavor profile, ingredients, and preparation methods. From the simple and classic to the more elaborate, we have something for everyone. Whether you are a seasoned cook or just starting out, these recipes will provide you with the knowledge and skills you need to create delicious and authentic Lebanese soups and salads at home. So, let's dive in and explore the wonderful world of Lebanese soups and salads!

Did you know that...

1. The word "fattoush" in Lebanese cuisine means "crumbled bread," and the dish is traditionally made with leftover pieces of pita bread.
2. Tabbouleh, a popular Lebanese salad, is typically made with parsley as the main ingredient and is considered one of the healthiest salads in the world.
3. The national dish of Lebanon is Kibbeh, a mixture of ground beef, bulgur wheat, and spices, that can be served raw, fried, or baked.
4. Lentil soup, or "ads," is a staple in Lebanese cuisine and is often served as a first course during formal meals.
5. Fattoush and tabbouleh are often served together in Lebanese restaurants, as the combination of fresh greens and crunchy pita chips creates a perfect balance of flavors and textures.
6. The traditional Lebanese salad called "Raita" is made with yogurt, cucumbers, and mint, and is a refreshing side dish to balance out spicy meals.
7. In Lebanese cuisine, soups are often served with a side of rice, making them a filling and satisfying meal.
8. The use of mint and parsley is a common ingredient in Lebanese soups and salads, adding a fresh and bright flavor to the dishes.
9. A popular variation of lentil soup in Lebanese cuisine is made with lemon and cumin, adding a tangy and spicy flavor to the dish.
10. The Lebanese salad "Laban bi Khodra," meaning "yogurt with greens," is made with yogurt, herbs, and vegetables, and is a popular vegan dish in Lebanese cuisine.

Baba Ghanoush Salad

Baba Ghanoush is a popular Lebanese dip made from roasted eggplant, tahini, lemon juice, and spices. This flavorful and creamy dip is traditionally served as an appetizer, but it can also be served as a salad for a more substantial meal. The dish is believed to have originated in the Eastern Mediterranean and has been enjoyed for centuries.

 4 SERVINGS 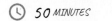 50 MINUTES 150 KCAL  EASY

INGREDIENTS

- 2 medium eggplants
- 1/4 cup tahini
- 2 cloves of garlic, minced
- 2 tablespoons of lemon juice
- 2 tablespoons of olive oil
- Salt, to taste
- Paprika, for garnish

DIRECTIONS

1. Preheat your oven to 400°F.
2. Wash and dry the eggplants. Using a fork, poke holes all over the eggplants. Place the eggplants on a baking sheet and roast in the oven for 25 minutes or until they are soft and slightly charred.
3. Allow the eggplants to cool completely. Cut the eggplants in half and scoop out the flesh into a food processor.
4. Add the tahini, minced garlic, lemon juice, and olive oil to the food processor. Season with salt to taste.
5. Blend the ingredients until smooth and creamy. If the mixture is too thick, add a little bit of water to thin it out.
6. Transfer the mixture to a serving bowl. Drizzle with a little bit of olive oil and sprinkle with paprika for garnish.
7. Serve the Baba Ghanoush salad as a dip with pita chips or as a salad with fresh vegetables.

Enjoy this flavorful and creamy Roasted Eggplant Salad! The smoky flavor of the roasted eggplant pairs perfectly with the tangy lemon juice and nutty tahini. Serve this dish as a dip with pita chips or as a salad with fresh vegetables for a healthy and satisfying meal.

Shorbat Brokli wa Jibne

Broccoli and cheese soup is a hearty and comforting dish that is popular in Lebanese cuisine. This creamy soup combines tender broccoli florets with melted cheese, creating a rich and flavorful meal that is perfect for a cold winter day. The dish is believed to have been influenced by European cuisine and has become a staple in Lebanese households.

 4 SERVINGS  45 MINUTES 400 KCAL  EASY

INGREDIENTS

- 1 head of broccoli, chopped into florets
- 1 onion, chopped
- 3 cloves of garlic, minced
- 4 cups of chicken or vegetable broth
- 1 cup of heavy cream
- 1 cup of grated cheddar cheese
- Salt and pepper, to taste
- Croutons, for garnish

DIRECTIONS

1. In a large pot, heat 1 tablespoon of olive oil over medium heat. Add the chopped onions and minced garlic, and cook until the onions are soft and translucent, about 5 minutes.
2. Add the broccoli florets to the pot and cook for another 5 minutes, stirring occasionally.
3. Pour in the broth and bring to a boil. Reduce the heat to low and let the soup simmer for 10 minutes, or until the broccoli is tender.
4. Remove the pot from heat and use an immersion blender or transfer the soup to a blender and puree until smooth.
5. Return the pureed soup to the pot and stir in the heavy cream. Heat over low heat until the soup is heated through, but do not let it boil.
6. Stir in the grated cheddar cheese until melted and well combined. Season with salt and pepper to taste.
7. Serve the Broccoli and Cheese Soup hot, garnished with croutons.

This Broccoli and Cheese Soup is a warm and comforting meal that is perfect for a cold winter day. The creamy cheese and tender broccoli make for a delicious and satisfying soup that is sure to become a family favorite. Serve this soup with a side of crusty bread or croutons for a complete meal.

Salatet Remoosh

Beetroot Salad is a colorful and flavorful dish that is a staple in Lebanese cuisine. Made with cooked beetroot, parsley, mint, and a tangy lemon dressing, this salad is light and refreshing, making it the perfect side dish for any meal. Beetroot has a long history in Lebanese cuisine, with references to the vegetable being used in cooking dating back to the Ottoman Empire.

🍴 **4** SERVINGS   🕐 **60** MINUTES   ⚖️ **150** KCAL   ☆ EASY

INGREDIENTS

- 4 medium beetroot, peeled and diced
- 1 cup chopped parsley
- 1 cup chopped mint
- 1 lemon, juiced
- 2 tablespoons olive oil
- Salt and pepper, to taste

DIRECTIONS

1. Preheat the oven to 400°F. Wrap the diced beetroot in foil and bake in the oven for 45 minutes, or until tender.
2. Remove the beetroot from the oven and let it cool.
3. In a large bowl, combine the cooked beetroot, chopped parsley, and chopped mint.
4. In a separate small bowl, whisk together the lemon juice and olive oil.
5. Pour the lemon dressing over the beetroot mixture and stir to combine. Season with salt and pepper to taste.
6. Chill the salad in the refrigerator for 30 minutes to allow the flavors to meld together.
7. Serve the Beetroot Salad chilled, garnished with additional chopped parsley and mint, if desired.

This Beetroot Salad is a refreshing and flavorful side dish that is perfect for any meal. The bright red color of the beetroot is eye-catching and the tangy lemon dressing complements the earthy flavor of the beets perfectly. Whether you're serving it with grilled chicken, fish, or tofu, this salad is sure to be a hit with everyone at the table.

Salatet Zozeir

Carrot and Lemon Salad is a classic Lebanese dish that is simple to make yet packed with flavor. With its bright orange color and zesty lemon dressing, this salad is both visually appealing and delicious. Carrots have a long history in Lebanese cuisine, with the vegetable being cultivated in the country for centuries.

 4 SERVINGS 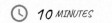 10 MINUTES 75 KCAL  EASY

INGREDIENTS

- 4 medium carrots, grated
- 1 lemon, juiced
- 2 tablespoons olive oil
- Salt and pepper, to taste
- Fresh parsley, chopped (optional)

DIRECTIONS

1. In a large bowl, combine the grated carrots.
2. In a separate small bowl, whisk together the lemon juice and olive oil.
3. Pour the lemon dressing over the grated carrots and stir to combine. Season with salt and pepper to taste.
4. Chill the salad in the refrigerator for 30 minutes to allow the flavors to meld together.
5. Serve the Carrot and Lemon Salad chilled, garnished with chopped parsley, if desired.

This Carrot and Lemon Salad is a fresh and flavorful side dish that is perfect for any meal. The lemon dressing provides a tangy contrast to the sweetness of the carrots, making this salad a crowd-pleaser. Whether you're serving it with grilled chicken, fish, or tofu, this salad is sure to be a hit with everyone at the table.

Shorbat Djaj

Chicken and Rice Soup, also known as Shorbat Djaj, is a traditional Lebanese soup that is both nourishing and delicious. This soup is a staple in many households, and it is often served for lunch or dinner. The simple combination of chicken, rice, and vegetables makes for a comforting and satisfying meal that is sure to please everyone at the table.

 4 SERVINGS   40 MINUTES   300 KCAL  EASY

INGREDIENTS

- 1 pound boneless, skinless chicken breast, cut into bite-sized pieces
- 1 onion, chopped
- 2 garlic cloves, minced
- 2 carrots, diced
- 2 celery stalks, diced
- 1 cup long-grain rice
- 8 cups chicken broth
- 1 teaspoon dried thyme
- 1 teaspoon dried basil
- Salt and pepper, to taste

DIRECTIONS

1. In a large saucepan, heat a small amount of oil over medium heat. Add the chicken and cook until browned on all sides. Remove the chicken from the pan and set aside.
2. In the same saucepan, add the onion, garlic, carrots, and celery and cook until softened, about 5 minutes.
3. Stir in the rice and cook for 2 minutes, or until lightly toasted.
4. Add the chicken broth, thyme, basil, salt, and pepper to the saucepan and bring to a boil.
5. Reduce the heat to low and return the chicken to the pan. Simmer for 20 minutes, or until the rice is tender and the chicken is cooked through.
6. Serve the Chicken and Rice Soup hot, garnished with additional thyme and basil, if desired.

Shorbat Djaj is a simple and versatile soup that can be customized to suit your tastes. For a creamier soup, you can add a cup of heavy cream or half-and-half during the cooking process. For a vegetarian version, you can replace the chicken with diced potatoes or mushrooms. No matter how you make it, Shorbat Djaj is a comforting and delicious soup that is perfect for any day of the week.

Jameed

Lebanese Yogurt Soup, also known as Jameed, is a classic soup made from sheep's milk yogurt, wheat, and a variety of spices. This soup is believed to have originated in the mountainous regions of Lebanon, where the cold climate made it a perfect dish for warming up during the winter months. Today, Jameed is enjoyed all over Lebanon and is a staple in many households.

 4 SERVINGS 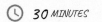 30 MINUTES 170 KCAL  EASY

INGREDIENTS

- 2 cups sheep's milk yogurt
- 2 cups water
- 1 cup dry wheat, soaked in water overnight
- 1 onion, finely chopped
- 3 garlic cloves, minced
- 1 teaspoon dried mint
- 1 teaspoon ground cumin
- Salt and pepper, to taste

DIRECTIONS

1. In a large saucepan, bring the water to a boil.
2. Add the soaked wheat to the boiling water and cook for 10 minutes, or until tender.
3. In a separate saucepan, heat the onion and garlic in a small amount of oil until softened.
4. Add the cooked wheat to the saucepan with the onions and garlic and stir to combine.
5. Stir in the sheep's milk yogurt, mint, cumin, salt, and pepper. Cook for 5 minutes, or until heated through.
6. Serve the Lebanese Yogurt Soup hot, garnished with additional mint and cumin, if desired.

This creamy and comforting soup is a great way to warm up on a chilly day. The combination of yogurt, wheat, and spices makes for a filling and nutritious meal that is easy to prepare. Jameed can be served as a main course or as a starter, and it pairs well with a variety of dishes, such as grilled meats and vegetables. Whether you're a fan of traditional Lebanese cuisine or simply looking for a new soup recipe, Jameed is sure to be a hit.

CHAPTER 3

Meat dishes

Meat dishes are a staple in Lebanese cuisine, featuring a variety of flavors, textures, and cooking methods that make them a staple in every household. The love for meat dishes in Lebanese cuisine is evident in its rich history, with traditional dishes dating back centuries, passed down from generation to generation. The country's diverse geography, which encompasses fertile valleys, high mountain ranges, and coastal plains, provides a variety of meats, including lamb, beef, poultry, and game.

Lebanese cuisine is characterized by the use of simple ingredients, such as olive oil, lemon juice, herbs, and spices, which enhance the flavor of the meat. The meat dishes range from slow-cooked stews to griddled kebabs, and they are typically served with rice, vegetables, or bread, providing a well-balanced meal.

One of the most famous meat dishes in Lebanese cuisine is Kibbeh, a mix of ground meat and bulgur wheat, shaped into balls or patties and served either fried or baked. Another well-known dish is Shish Tawook, a popular street food made from marinated chicken skewers grilled to perfection. For those who love slow-cooked meals, there's the famous Musakhan, a tender roasted chicken dish flavored with spices, onions, and pine nuts, served with traditional Arabic bread.

The love for meat dishes in Lebanese cuisine is not limited to just traditional dishes. Today, there are numerous variations and innovations of classic dishes, providing a range of options for everyone to enjoy. Whether you prefer a classic recipe or a modern twist, there's something for everyone in the world of Lebanese meat dishes.

So, in this chapter, we will explore some of the most popular meat dishes in Lebanese cuisine, with recipes that range from traditional to contemporary, providing a comprehensive guide to cooking delicious and satisfying meat-based meals. So, get your aprons ready and let's delve into the world of Lebanese meat dishes!

Did you know that...

1. The traditional Lebanese meat dish "Kebab" (Grilled meat skewers) has its roots in ancient Persia.
2. "Shawarma" is a popular street food in Lebanon and many other Middle Eastern countries.
3. "Mansaf" is considered the national dish of Jordan but is also popular in Lebanon.
4. "Lahm bi Ajeen", a type of meat pizza, is a common dish served in Lebanese households and restaurants.
5. "Kibbeh", a dish made of ground meat, bulgur wheat and spices, is a staple in Lebanese cuisine.
6. "Arayes", a sandwich filled with spiced meat, is a popular snack food in Lebanon.
7. "Fattoush" is a popular salad that often includes diced pieces of grilled meat, such as chicken or lamb.
8. "Kofta", meatballs made from a mixture of ground meat, spices, and sometimes bulgur wheat, are a staple in Lebanese cuisine.
9. "Sfiha", a Lebanese version of a meat pie, is often served as a snack or light meal.
10. "Tabbouleh", a popular Lebanese salad, often includes small pieces of grilled or boiled chicken or lamb as a protein source.

Shish Taouk

Shish Taouk is a popular Lebanese dish of marinated chicken that is skewered and grilled to perfection. This dish is believed to have originated in Ottoman Turkey and was introduced to the Middle East by soldiers who brought the technique back with them.

 4 SERVINGS   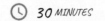 30 MINUTES   400 KCAL    EASY

INGREDIENTS

- 1 pound boneless chicken breast, cut into 1-inch cubes
- 3 cloves garlic, minced
- 1/4 cup lemon juice
- 1/4 cup olive oil
- 1 teaspoon salt
- 1 teaspoon paprika
- 1 teaspoon cumin
- 1/2 teaspoon black pepper
- 8 metal skewers or bamboo skewers (soaked in water for 30 minutes)

DIRECTIONS

1. In a large bowl, whisk together the garlic, lemon juice, olive oil, salt, paprika, cumin, and black pepper.
2. Add the chicken cubes and mix until they are evenly coated with the marinade.
3. Cover the bowl with plastic wrap and refrigerate for at least 30 minutes, or up to 8 hours.
4. Preheat a grill or grill pan to medium-high heat.
5. Skewer the chicken cubes, spacing them evenly on the skewer.
6. Grill the kebabs for 8-10 minutes on each side, or until the chicken is cooked through and the outside is lightly charred.
7. Serve the kebabs hot with rice or bread, and a side of vegetables or salad.

Shish Taouk is a delicious and easy to make dish that is perfect for outdoor barbecues or as a weeknight dinner. The tender chicken and flavorful marinade make for a satisfying meal that is sure to be a crowd-pleaser. Try serving the kebabs with a tangy yogurt sauce for an extra burst of flavor!

Kofta Arayes

A traditional Middle Eastern dish, Grilled Lamb Chops (Kofta Arayes) is a delicious and savory combination of seasoned ground lamb wrapped in a thin, crispy pita bread. This dish has a rich history, originating in the Lebanon and surrounding areas, where it has been enjoyed for centuries as a staple food during celebrations and special occasions.

 4 SERVINGS   45 MINUTES   600 KCAL   MED

INGREDIENTS

- 1 pound ground lamb
- 1 small onion, finely chopped
- 3 cloves garlic, minced
- 1 teaspoon ground cumin
- 1 teaspoon paprika
- 1/2 teaspoon ground coriander
- 1/2 teaspoon allspice
- Salt and pepper, to taste
- 4 thin pita breads
- Olive oil, for brushing

DIRECTIONS

1. Let's start by making the filling for our Grilled Lamb Chops (Kofta Arayes). In a large mixing bowl, combine 1 pound of ground lamb with 1 finely chopped small onion, 3 minced cloves of garlic, 1 teaspoon of ground cumin, 1 teaspoon of paprika, 1/2 teaspoon of ground coriander, 1/2 teaspoon of allspice, and a pinch of salt and pepper.
2. Use your hands to mix all of the ingredients together until they are well combined. This is a great opportunity to get a little messy and have some fun in the kitchen!
3. Divide the mixture into 4 equal portions and shape each portion into a sausage shape. This will be the filling for our pita bread wraps.
4. Next, grab 4 thin pita breads and place one sausage shape onto each pita bread.
5. Wrap the pita bread tightly around the sausage shape, making sure to seal the edges so the filling stays inside. Repeat this step with the remaining pita breads and sausage shapes.
6. Time to grill! Heat up a grill or grill pan to medium-high heat and brush the outside of the pita bread wraps with a little olive oil. This will help them get nice and crispy.
7. Place the pita bread wraps on the grill or grill pan and grill for about 3-5 minutes on each side, or until they are crispy and the lamb filling is fully cooked. Keep an eye on them to make sure they don't burn!

Kafta Kebab

Kafta kebab is a popular dish in Lebanese cuisine, made with ground beef mixed with spices, onions, and parsley. This dish has been enjoyed in the Middle East for centuries and is a staple at Lebanese barbecues and celebrations.

6 SERVINGS   **35** MINUTES   **200** KCAL   EASY

INGREDIENTS

- 1 lb. ground beef
- 1 large onion, finely chopped
- 1/4 cup parsley, chopped
- 2 garlic cloves, minced
- 1 tsp. salt
- 1 tsp. black pepper
- 1 tsp. allspice
- 2 tbsp. olive oil
- 6 metal or wooden skewers

DIRECTIONS

1. In a large bowl, mix the ground beef with the chopped onions, parsley, minced garlic, salt, pepper, and allspice.
2. Divide the mixture into 6 equal portions and shape each portion into a sausage shape around the skewer.
3. Preheat a grill or grill pan to medium-high heat.
4. Brush the kebabs with olive oil and place them on the hot grill.
5. Cook for 7-8 minutes on each side or until fully cooked through and browned on the outside.
6. Serve hot with pita bread and tahini sauce.

Kafta kebab is a delicious and easy dish that is perfect for family gatherings and special events. The blend of spices, herbs, and tender ground beef creates a flavorful and juicy kebab that is sure to impress your guests. So, next time you're looking for a quick and tasty Lebanese meal, give kafta kebab a try!

Lamb Shawarma

A popular street food in the Middle East, Lamb Shawarma is a delicious wrap filled with tender, juicy slices of marinated lamb, crisp veggies, and tangy sauces. This dish has a rich history, tracing its roots back to the Ottoman Empire and has since become a staple in Lebanese cuisine.

 4 SERVINGS   30 MINUTES   🏋 700 KCAL   ☆ MED

INGREDIENTS

- 2 pounds boneless lamb leg, sliced thin
- 1/2 cup plain Greek yogurt
- 1/4 cup lemon juice
- 2 cloves garlic, minced
- 1 teaspoon ground cumin
- 1 teaspoon paprika
- 1/2 teaspoon ground coriander
- Salt and pepper, to taste
- 4 large flatbreads (pita bread or lavash bread)
- 1 large tomato, sliced
- 1 large cucumber, sliced
- 1 small red onion, sliced
- 1 cup hummus
- 1/2 cup tahini sauce

DIRECTIONS

1. In a large bowl, mix together the sliced lamb, yogurt, lemon juice, garlic, cumin, paprika, coriander, salt, and pepper.
2. Cover and refrigerate for at least 1 hour, or up to 4 hours, to allow the flavors to marinate.
3. Heat a grill or grill pan to medium-high heat.
4. Remove the lamb from the refrigerator and place it on the grill or grill pan.
5. Grill the lamb for 3-4 minutes on each side, or until it is cooked through and browned.
6. To assemble the shawarma, spread a generous amount of hummus on each flatbread.
7. Place the grilled lamb on top of the hummus, followed by slices of tomato, cucumber, and red onion.
8. Roll up the flatbread to enclose the filling.
9. Serve the Lamb Shawarma hot, garnished with a drizzle of tahini sauce and extra sliced veggies, if desired.

Note: For a crunchier shawarma, place the assembled wrap in a hot skillet for a minute or two on each side, until it is crispy and slightly charred.

Shish Taouk

A staple in Lebanese cuisine, Shish Taouk is a delicious dish made of tender, juicy marinated chicken skewers grilled to perfection. This dish has a rich history, dating back to medieval times when it was a popular street food. Today, it remains a popular choice for a quick and satisfying meal.

🍴 *4 SERVINGS*   🕐 *30 MINUTES*   ⚖️ *350 KCAL*   ☆ *EASY*

INGREDIENTS

- 2 pounds boneless, skinless chicken breast, cut into 1-inch pieces
- 1/2 cup plain Greek yogurt
- 1/4 cup lemon juice
- 2 cloves garlic, minced
- 1 teaspoon ground cumin
- 1 teaspoon paprika
- 1/2 teaspoon ground coriander
- Salt and pepper, to taste
- 1 large red bell pepper, sliced
- 1 large onion, sliced
- 4 skewers
- 1/2 cup tahini sauce

DIRECTIONS

1. In a large bowl, mix together the chicken, yogurt, lemon juice, garlic, cumin, paprika, coriander, salt, and pepper.
2. Cover and refrigerate for at least 1 hour, or up to 4 hours, to allow the flavors to marinate.
3. Heat a grill or grill pan to medium-high heat.
4. Remove the chicken from the refrigerator and thread it onto skewers, alternating with slices of red bell pepper and onion.
5. Place the skewers on the grill or grill pan and grill for 10-12 minutes, turning occasionally, until the chicken is cooked through and browned.
6. Serve the Grilled Chicken Skewers hot, garnished with a drizzle of tahini sauce and extra lemon wedges, if desired.

Note: If using wooden skewers, soak them in water for 30 minutes before grilling to prevent burning.

Kibbeh Bil Sanieh

Kibbeh Bil Sanieh is a classic Lebanese dish that combines seasoned lamb, spices, and rice in a layered casserole, baked until golden and crispy. This dish is believed to have originated in the Middle East and has been a staple in Lebanese cuisine for centuries. The combination of tender lamb, aromatic spices, and fluffy rice creates a delicious and satisfying meal.

4 SERVINGS   **90** MINUTES   **550** KCAL   MED

INGREDIENTS

- 1 pound ground lamb
- 1 cup fine bulgur wheat
- 1 medium onion, grated
- 1 teaspoon allspice
- 1 teaspoon cinnamon
- 1 teaspoon ground coriander
- Salt and pepper, to taste
- 2 tablespoons olive oil
- 2 cups chicken broth
- 1 cup long-grain white rice
- 1/2 cup pine nuts
- 2 tablespoons butter
- 2 tablespoons chopped parsley
- 2 tablespoons chopped mint

DIRECTIONS

1. In a large bowl, mix together the lamb, bulgur wheat, grated onion, allspice, cinnamon, coriander, salt, and pepper.
2. Knead the mixture until well combined and smooth, then set aside.
3. In a large skillet, heat the olive oil over medium heat. Add the lamb mixture and cook, stirring frequently, until browned and fully cooked, about 10 minutes.
4. Stir in the chicken broth and bring to a boil, then reduce heat to low and cook for an additional 5 minutes.
5. In a separate pot, cook the rice according to package instructions.
6. In a large baking dish, layer the lamb mixture, cooked rice, and pine nuts.
7. Dot with butter and sprinkle with parsley and mint.
8. Bake at 350°F (180°C) for 30 minutes, or until golden and crispy.
9. Serve the Kibbeh Bil Sanieh hot, garnished with additional herbs and a squeeze of lemon, if desired.

CHAPTER 4

Fish dishes

Lebanese cuisine is a unique blend of flavors and spices that has been passed down from generations to generations. It is a reflection of the rich cultural and historical heritage of the country and its people. With its extensive coastline along the Mediterranean, it's no surprise that seafood is a staple in Lebanese cuisine. From grilled fish to fried calamari, there's no shortage of delicious fish dishes to be found in Lebanon.

Fish dishes have always been an important part of Lebanese cuisine, not just for their taste and flavor but also for their health benefits. With a variety of fish and seafood options, there's a fish dish for every taste. Whether it's the delicate flavor of baked sole, the robust taste of grilled salmon, or the tangy flavor of lemon and garlic-marinated shrimp, fish dishes in Lebanese cuisine are both delicious and nutritious.

In this book, we have compiled some of the best and most popular fish dishes from Lebanon. Each dish is unique in its own way, with its own blend of spices, herbs, and seasonings, and each one is sure to leave a lasting impression on your taste buds. Whether you're an experienced cook or a beginner, this book will guide you through the steps of creating authentic and delicious Lebanese fish dishes that you can enjoy in the comfort of your own home.

From the classic Lebanese-style grilled fish to the delicious Fried Calamari with Tahini Sauce, you'll find a dish for every occasion. Whether you're looking for a quick and easy weeknight dinner or a more elaborate feast, this book has got you covered. Each recipe is accompanied by clear and concise instructions, making it easy to follow and prepare, even for those with limited cooking experience.

So, whether you're a fan of seafood or simply looking to try something new, this book is the perfect guide to the world of Lebanese fish dishes. Let's dive in and discover the delicious world of Lebanese cuisine!

Did you know that...

1. The traditional Lebanese meat dish "Kebab" (Grilled meat skewers) has its roots in ancient Persia.
2. "Shawarma" is a popular street food in Lebanon and many other Middle Eastern countries.
3. "Mansaf" is considered the national dish of Jordan but is also popular in Lebanon.
4. "Lahm bi Ajeen", a type of meat pizza, is a common dish served in Lebanese households and restaurants.
5. "Kibbeh", a dish made of ground meat, bulgur wheat and spices, is a staple in Lebanese cuisine.
6. "Arayes", a sandwich filled with spiced meat, is a popular snack food in Lebanon.
7. "Fattoush" is a popular salad that often includes diced pieces of grilled meat, such as chicken or lamb.
8. "Kofta", meatballs made from a mixture of ground meat, spices, and sometimes bulgur wheat, are a staple in Lebanese cuisine.
9. "Sfiha", a Lebanese version of a meat pie, is often served as a snack or light meal.
10. "Tabbouleh", a popular Lebanese salad, often includes small pieces of grilled or boiled chicken or lamb as a protein source.

Qalamari Meshwi

This classic Lebanese dish is a crowd-pleaser, consisting of tender and crispy calamari rings coated in a light batter and deep-fried until golden brown. The dish is traditionally served with a squeeze of lemon and a side of tahini sauce for dipping.

 4 SERVINGS  30 MINUTES 600 KCAL  EASY

INGREDIENTS

- 2 lbs calamari, cleaned and cut into rings
- 2 cups all-purpose flour
- 2 tsp salt
- 1 tsp paprika
- 1 tsp black pepper
- 1 tsp dried oregano
- 1 tsp dried basil
- 1 tsp dried thyme
- Vegetable oil, for frying
- Lemon wedges, for serving
- Tahini sauce, for serving

DIRECTIONS

1. In a large bowl, mix together the flour, salt, paprika, black pepper, oregano, basil, and thyme.
2. Dip each calamari ring into the flour mixture, making sure it's fully coated.
3. In a large saucepan, heat the vegetable oil over medium heat until it reaches 375°F.
4. Carefully drop the calamari rings into the hot oil and fry for 2-3 minutes, or until golden brown.
5. Remove the fried calamari from the oil using a slotted spoon and place on a paper towel-lined plate to drain excess oil.
6. Serve the fried calamari hot with lemon wedges and tahini sauce for dipping.

Fried calamari is a quick and easy dish to make, perfect for serving at a party or as a casual weeknight meal. The tender and crispy texture of the calamari combined with the tangy lemon and rich tahini sauce make for a truly delicious dish.

Samak Meshwi

This popular Lebanese dish is a fresh and flavorful way to enjoy fresh sole. The fish is seasoned with a mix of spices, lemon juice, and olive oil, then grilled to perfection for a crispy exterior and flaky, tender interior.

4 SERVINGS   30 MINUTES   300 KCAL   EASY

INGREDIENTS

- 4 sole fillets (about 1 lb total)
- 2 tbsp olive oil
- 2 cloves garlic, minced
- 1 lemon, juiced
- 1 tsp paprika
- 1 tsp dried oregano
- 1 tsp dried basil
- 1 tsp dried thyme
- Salt and black pepper, to taste

DIRECTIONS

1. In a small bowl, whisk together the olive oil, garlic, lemon juice, paprika, oregano, basil, thyme, salt, and black pepper.
2. Place the sole fillets in a large shallow dish and pour the marinade over the top.
3. Cover the dish with plastic wrap and refrigerate for at least 30 minutes, or up to 2 hours.
4. Preheat your grill to high heat.
5. Lightly oil the grates of the grill.
6. Remove the sole from the marinade and discard the remaining marinade.
7. Place the sole fillets on the hot grill and cook for 3-4 minutes per side, or until the fish is opaque and easily flakes with a fork.
8. Serve the grilled sole hot with a squeeze of lemon and a side of your choice.

Grilled sole is a light and healthy option for a summertime meal. The combination of fresh fish, tangy lemon, and bold spices make for a delicious and satisfying dish. Serve it with a simple side of grilled vegetables or a fresh green salad for a complete meal.

Samak Mahshi

Stuffed Sole, also known as Samak Mahshi, is a classic Lebanese dish that is both flavorful and healthy. Sole is a delicate white fish that is stuffed with a mixture of spices, herbs, and rice. This dish is perfect for a family meal or special occasion, and it is sure to impress. With its flaky, tender fish and its aromatic stuffing, Stuffed Sole is a dish that is sure to satisfy.

4 SERVINGS   **60 MINUTES**   **350 KCAL**   **MED**

INGREDIENTS

- 4 whole soles, deboned and skinned
- 1 cup long-grain rice
- 1 onion, chopped
- 2 cloves garlic, minced
- 1 tsp. ground coriander
- 1 tsp. ground cumin
- 1 tsp. paprika
- 1 tsp. dried mint
- Salt and pepper, to taste
- 1/2 cup chopped fresh parsley
- 1/2 cup chopped fresh cilantro
- 1 lemon, sliced
- Olive oil, for drizzling

DIRECTIONS

1. In a large saucepan, cook the rice according to package instructions. Once done, set aside.
2. In a pan, sauté the onions and garlic until softened. Add the spices, dried mint, salt, and pepper, and cook for 2-3 minutes.
3. Add the cooked rice to the pan and mix well. Stir in the chopped parsley and cilantro, and set aside.
4. Preheat the oven to 400°F.
5. Season the deboned and skinned soles with salt and pepper, inside and out.
6. Spoon the rice mixture into each sole, and carefully close the fish to form a tight bundle.
7. Arrange the stuffed soles in a large baking dish, and place a lemon slice on top of each one.
8. Drizzle with olive oil, and bake in the oven for 25-30 minutes, or until the fish is cooked through and the top is golden brown.
9. Serve hot, garnished with lemon wedges and additional fresh herbs, if desired.

Samak Bil Khodra

Baked Red Snapper is a traditional Lebanese dish that is enjoyed by many families in the Middle East. It is a simple, yet flavorful dish that is made by baking fresh red snapper in a mixture of tomatoes, garlic, onions, and spices. This dish has a rich history in the Middle East and is a staple of Lebanese cuisine.

 4 SERVINGS  50 MINUTES 250 KCAL 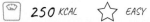 EASY

INGREDIENTS

- 4 whole red snapper, scaled and cleaned
- 4 ripe tomatoes, chopped
- 2 medium onions, chopped
- 4 garlic cloves, minced
- 1 teaspoon paprika
- 1 teaspoon ground cumin
- Salt and pepper to taste
- 3 tablespoons olive oil
- 1 lemon, sliced
- Fresh parsley leaves, chopped (optional)

DIRECTIONS

1. In a large saucepan, cook the rice according to package instructions. Once done, set aside.
2. In a pan, sauté the onions and garlic until softened. Add the spices, dried mint, salt, and pepper, and cook for 2-3 minutes.
3. Add the cooked rice to the pan and mix well. Stir in the chopped parsley and cilantro, and set aside.
4. Preheat the oven to 400°F.
5. Season the deboned and skinned soles with salt and pepper, inside and out.
6. Spoon the rice mixture into each sole, and carefully close the fish to form a tight bundle.
7. Arrange the stuffed soles in a large baking dish, and place a lemon slice on top of each one.
8. Drizzle with olive oil, and bake in the oven for 25-30 minutes, or until the fish is cooked through and the top is golden brown.
9. Serve hot, garnished with lemon wedges and additional fresh herbs, if desired.

Jebneh Scampi

A rich and flavorful dish, Shrimp Scampi is a staple of Lebanese cuisine. This dish is a combination of succulent shrimp, garlic, and a tangy lemon butter sauce. It is a popular dish along the Mediterranean coast and has been enjoyed for generations.

4 SERVINGS   20 MINUTES   300 KCAL   EASY

INGREDIENTS

- 1 lb large shrimp, peeled and deveined
- 6 cloves garlic, minced
- 1/4 cup lemon juice
- 1/4 cup butter
- 1/4 cup extra-virgin olive oil
- Salt and pepper, to taste
- Fresh parsley, chopped for garnish

DIRECTIONS

1. Preheat the oven to 425°F.
2. In a large skillet, heat the olive oil over medium heat. Add the minced garlic and cook until fragrant, about 1-2 minutes.
3. Add the shrimp to the skillet and season with salt and pepper. Cook until the shrimp turns pink, about 2-3 minutes.
4. Remove the shrimp from the skillet and set aside.
5. In the same skillet, add the lemon juice, butter, and a pinch of salt and pepper. Cook until the butter is melted, about 2 minutes.
6. Return the cooked shrimp to the skillet and gently toss with the lemon butter sauce.
7. Transfer the shrimp and sauce to a baking dish and place in the oven. Bake for 10 minutes, or until the shrimp are fully cooked and the sauce is hot.
8. Serve the shrimp scampi hot, garnished with chopped fresh parsley.

Barri Meshwi

Barri Meshwi, or grilled sea bass, is a popular fish dish in Lebanese cuisine, typically enjoyed in the summer months. The fish is seasoned with spices and lemon juice and grilled to perfection, creating a juicy and flavorful dish that is both healthy and delicious.

4 SERVINGS   **30 MINUTES**   **200 KCAL**   **EASY**

INGREDIENTS

- 4 sea bass fillets
- 1 lemon, juiced
- 1 tsp cumin
- 1 tsp paprika
- 1 tsp garlic powder
- 1 tsp dried oregano
- Salt and pepper, to taste
- 2 tbsp olive oil

DIRECTIONS

1. Rinse the sea bass fillets and pat dry.
2. In a small bowl, mix together the lemon juice, cumin, paprika, garlic powder, oregano, salt, and pepper.
3. Place the fish in a large, shallow dish and pour the lemon and spice mixture over the top.
4. Let the fish marinate for 10-15 minutes in the refrigerator.
5. Preheat the grill to high heat.
6. Brush the sea bass fillets with olive oil and place them on the grill.
7. Grill the fish for about 7-8 minutes on each side, or until fully cooked through and lightly charred.
8. Serve the grilled sea bass with a side of your choice, such as grilled vegetables or a salad.
9. Enjoy the delicious flavors of the grilled sea bass and savor the juicy, flaky meat.

For a twist on this classic dish, try stuffing the sea bass with lemon slices and fresh herbs before grilling. Or, you can also add a splash of white wine to the marinade for a touch of sophistication. However you choose to enjoy it, this grilled sea bass is sure to be a hit with your guests and will become a staple in your seafood repertoire.

CHAPTER 5

Modern recipes

Welcome to the world of modern Lebanese cuisine! This collection of recipes showcases the contemporary twist on traditional dishes, bringing together a fusion of flavors and techniques to create unique and delicious meals.

Lebanese cuisine is renowned for its rich and diverse flavors, rooted in a rich history of hospitality and love for food. From mezze platters brimming with dips and spreads, to grilled meats and vegetables seasoned with spices and herbs, there is something for everyone in Lebanese cooking.

In this book, we explore the modern take on classic Lebanese dishes, incorporating global ingredients and contemporary cooking methods to create innovative and inspiring meals. With an emphasis on fresh, seasonal ingredients, each recipe is a celebration of the vibrant, bold and mouth-watering flavors of the Middle East.

Whether you are an experienced cook or just starting out in the kitchen, these recipes are easy to follow and guarantee delicious results. From quick and healthy weeknight dinners to impressive party dishes, this collection has something for every occasion.

So, grab your apron, fire up the grill and let's get cooking! Experience the taste of modern Lebanese cuisine, with a twist, in the comfort of your own home.

Did you know that...

1. Lebanese cuisine is widely considered to be one of the healthiest and most flavorful in the world.
2. Lebanese cuisine is heavily influenced by Mediterranean, Middle Eastern, and Ottoman cuisine.
3. Mezze is a staple of Lebanese cuisine and is a collection of small, flavorful dishes that are meant to be shared among friends and family.
4. Tabbouleh, a popular salad made with parsley, bulgur wheat, tomatoes, and lemon, is considered the national dish of Lebanon.
5. Lebanese bread, or pita bread, is a staple of Lebanese cuisine and is used in many dishes, including sandwiches and dipping sauces.
6. Lentils, chickpeas, and bulgur wheat are common ingredients in Lebanese cuisine and are used in a variety of dishes, including soups and stews.
7. Lebanese cuisine is known for its use of herbs and spices, including mint, parsley, cumin, and cinnamon.
8. Lebanese wine, particularly red wine, is becoming increasingly popular and is known for its high quality and full-bodied flavor.
9. Baklava, a sweet pastry made with layers of phyllo dough and honey, is a popular dessert in Lebanese cuisine and is often served with a glass of sweet Lebanese tea.
10. In Lebanese cuisine, food is considered a celebration of life and is often served family-style to encourage sharing and conversation.

Lebanese Grilled Eggplant with Yogurt Sauce

This dish is a popular vegetarian dish in Lebanese cuisine, known for its unique blend of flavors and textures. It has a long history in Lebanese culture, dating back to ancient times when eggplants were first cultivated in the region. The combination of grilled eggplant with a creamy yogurt sauce is a delicious and healthy dish that is easy to prepare and perfect for a summer barbeque or an outdoor meal with friends and family.

 4 SERVINGS   30 MINUTES   200 KCAL   EASY

INGREDIENTS

- 4 medium-sized eggplants
- 1 cup of Greek yogurt
- 2 cloves of garlic, minced
- 2 tablespoons of olive oil
- 1 teaspoon of salt
- 1/2 teaspoon of black pepper
- 1 teaspoon of dried mint
- 1 teaspoon of lemon juice
- 1 tablespoon of chopped parsley for garnish

DIRECTIONS

1. Preheat the grill to medium heat.
2. Cut the eggplants into 1/2 inch slices, and place them in a large bowl.
3. In a separate bowl, whisk together the yogurt, garlic, olive oil, salt, pepper, dried mint, and lemon juice.
4. Brush the eggplant slices with the yogurt mixture on both sides.
5. Place the eggplant slices on the grill and cook for about 3-5 minutes on each side, or until the eggplants are tender and slightly charred.
6. In the meantime, warm up the remaining yogurt sauce in a saucepan.
7. Serve the grilled eggplant slices on a serving platter and drizzle with the warm yogurt sauce.
8. Garnish with chopped parsley and serve immediately.

Lebanese-Style Quinoa Salad

This dish is a modern take on the classic Lebanese-style quinoa salad, made with a combination of fresh herbs and spices for a fresh, healthy and flavorful meal. In Lebanese cuisine, quinoa is used as an alternative to traditional grains like rice, bulgur, and barley. The dish is perfect for a light summer meal or as a healthy side dish.

🍴 *4 SERVINGS*   🕐 *30 MINUTES*   ⚖ *250 KCAL*   ☆ *EASY*

INGREDIENTS

- 1 cup uncooked quinoa
- 2 cups water
- 1 large cucumber, peeled, seeded, and chopped
- 1 large red bell pepper, chopped
- 1 cup cherry tomatoes, halved
- 1/4 cup fresh parsley, chopped
- 1/4 cup fresh mint, chopped
- 1/4 cup fresh cilantro, chopped
- 1/4 cup lemon juice
- 1/4 cup olive oil
- 1 teaspoon sumac
- 1/2 teaspoon salt
- 1/4 teaspoon black pepper

DIRECTIONS

1. Rinse quinoa thoroughly and drain. Add quinoa and water to a medium saucepan and bring to a boil.
2. Reduce heat to low, cover, and simmer for 15 minutes, or until all the water has been absorbed.
3. Remove from heat and let cool.
4. In a large bowl, combine the quinoa, cucumber, red bell pepper, cherry tomatoes, parsley, mint, and cilantro.
5. In a small bowl, whisk together lemon juice, olive oil, sumac, salt, and black pepper.
6. Pour the dressing over the quinoa mixture and toss to coat.
7. Serve at room temperature or chilled.

Kibbeh Nayyeh

Kibbeh Nayyeh is a traditional Lebanese dish made from raw ground lamb or beef mixed with bulgur wheat, spices, and sometimes mint. This dish is typically served as an appetizer and is a staple in Lebanese cuisine. In this modern take on the dish, we'll be using a blend of ground lamb and beef to create a more flavorful and healthier version of Kibbeh Nayyeh.

 4 SERVINGS   30 MINUTES   300 KCAL    MED

INGREDIENTS

- 1 pound ground lamb
- 1 pound ground beef
- 1 cup bulgur wheat
- 1 medium onion, minced
- 2 cloves garlic, minced
- 1 teaspoon ground cumin
- 1 teaspoon paprika
- 1/2 teaspoon allspice
- 1/2 teaspoon cinnamon
- 1/4 teaspoon nutmeg
- Salt and pepper, to taste
- 2 tablespoons olive oil
- 1/4 cup chopped fresh parsley
- 1/4 cup chopped fresh mint
- 1/4 cup pomegranate seeds
- 1/4 cup lemon juice

DIRECTIONS

1. In a large bowl, soak the bulgur wheat in water for 20 minutes.
2. In a food processor, puree the onion and garlic until smooth.
3. Add the ground lamb and beef to the food processor and pulse until well combined.
4. Transfer the mixture to the bowl with the soaked bulgur wheat and add in the spices, salt and pepper, olive oil, parsley, mint, pomegranate seeds, and lemon juice. Mix everything together until well combined.
5. With wet hands, form the mixture into small balls.
6. Arrange the kibbeh on a serving platter and garnish with extra parsley, mint, and pomegranate seeds.
7. Serve with lettuce leaves, pita bread, or crackers for dipping.

This modern take on Kibbeh Nayyeh offers a healthier and more flavorful twist on a traditional Lebanese dish. The combination of ground lamb and beef provides a rich, savory flavor, while the addition of bulgur wheat and spices creates a satisfying texture. The pomegranate seeds and lemon juice add a pop of freshness, making this dish the perfect appetizer for any dinner party or gathering.

Lebanese Roasted Vegetable Pita Sandwiches

Lebanese Roasted Vegetable Pita Sandwiches are a modern twist on a traditional Lebanese dish. This recipe combines the delicious and unique flavors of the Middle East with healthy and tasty ingredients. The pita sandwiches are filled with roasted vegetables, such as bell peppers, zucchini, and eggplant, and are topped with a tangy tahini sauce, adding a delightful texture to the dish.

 4 SERVINGS 35 MINUTES 450 KCAL  EASY

INGREDIENTS

- 4 large pita breads
- 2 large bell peppers (red and yellow), sliced
- 1 large zucchini, sliced
- 1 large eggplant, sliced
- 2 tablespoons of olive oil
- Salt and pepper to taste
- 1/2 cup of tahini
- 2 cloves of garlic, minced
- 2 tablespoons of lemon juice
- 2 tablespoons of water
- Fresh parsley for garnish

DIRECTIONS

1. Preheat oven to 400°F (200°C).
2. On a large baking sheet, place the sliced bell peppers, zucchini, and eggplant. Drizzle with olive oil and season with salt and pepper.
3. Roast in the oven for 20-25 minutes, or until the vegetables are slightly charred and tender.
4. In a medium bowl, whisk together the tahini, minced garlic, lemon juice, and water until the sauce is smooth. If the sauce is too thick, add a bit more water.
5. Cut the pita bread in half to create two rounds. Toast the pitas in a toaster or on a pan until slightly crispy.
6. Fill each pita half with the roasted vegetables and drizzle with the tahini sauce.
7. Garnish with fresh parsley and serve immediately. Enjoy your modern take on a classic Lebanese dish!

Lebanese Rice Pudding with Rose Water

Rice pudding is a beloved dessert across many cultures, and the Lebanese version is no exception. This sweet and creamy dish is infused with the fragrant flavor of rose water and sprinkled with cinnamon for a touch of warmth. This modern take on the traditional recipe uses a mixture of milk and cream for a richer and creamier pudding.

 4 SERVINGS 40 MINUTES 400 KCAL 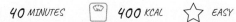 EASY

INGREDIENTS

- 1 cup of short-grain white rice
- 3 cups of milk
- 1 cup of heavy cream
- 1 cup of sugar
- 1 teaspoon of vanilla extract
- 1 teaspoon of rose water
- 1/4 teaspoon of cinnamon
- 1/4 teaspoon of salt
- Sliced almonds, for garnish (optional)

DIRECTIONS

1. Rinse the rice in a fine mesh strainer and place it in a medium saucepan.
2. Add 2 cups of water to the saucepan and bring to a boil over medium-high heat.
3. Reduce heat to low, cover the saucepan and let the rice simmer for 18-20 minutes or until the water is fully absorbed.
4. In a separate saucepan, heat the milk and cream over medium heat until just warm.
5. Add the sugar, vanilla extract, rose water, cinnamon, and salt to the saucepan and stir until the sugar has dissolved.
6. Stir in the cooked rice into the milk mixture and continue to cook over low heat, stirring occasionally, for 20-25 minutes or until the pudding has thickened.
7. Remove the pudding from heat and let it cool slightly.
8. Pour the pudding into individual serving dishes or a large serving dish.
9. Sprinkle with sliced almonds, if using, and let the pudding cool to room temperature before serving. Serve chilled or at room temperature.

CHAPTER 6

Desserts

Lebanese cuisine is known for its diverse and rich flavors, and its desserts are no exception. From sweet and syrupy pastries to creamy and comforting puddings, Lebanese desserts are a celebration of flavor, texture, and tradition.

In Lebanon, desserts are not just a way to end a meal, they are also a symbol of hospitality and generosity. It is not uncommon to be offered a sweet treat when visiting someone's home, and serving a variety of desserts during special occasions such as weddings, religious festivals, and other celebrations is considered a sign of abundance and good fortune.

The ingredients used in Lebanese desserts are simple, yet carefully selected for their quality and flavor. Common ingredients include fresh and dried fruits, nuts, honey, sugar, and dairy products such as milk, yogurt, and clotted cream. Spices and aromatics such as cinnamon, vanilla, and rose water are also used to add depth and complexity to the desserts.

One of the defining characteristics of Lebanese desserts is their use of syrup, which is often made from sugar, water, and lemon juice. The syrup is drizzled over pastries and cakes to add sweetness and moisture, and to help preserve them. This tradition of using syrup in desserts is thought to have its roots in ancient Persia, where sugar was first cultivated and used as a sweetener.

Another important aspect of Lebanese desserts is the use of phyllo dough, which is used to make flaky and crispy pastries such as baklava and mamoul. The art of making phyllo dough is a labor-intensive process that requires patience and skill, and it is often passed down from generation to generation.

Lebanese desserts are not just delicious, they are also visually stunning. The use of vibrant colors, intricate designs, and delicate shapes is an expression of the creativity and pride that goes into every dessert.

Whether you are a fan of rich and creamy puddings, flaky and syrupy pastries, or crunchy and nutty cakes, you are sure to find a dessert in this book that will satisfy your sweet tooth. So, let's dive into the world of Lebanese desserts and discover the delicious and timeless treats that have been enjoyed by generations of families and friends.

Did you know that...

1. The famous Lebanese dessert "Mouhalabieh" is a traditional pudding made from rose water, orange blossom water, and milk.
2. "Baklava" is a sweet pastry that has been a staple of Lebanese cuisine for over a thousand years.
3. The sweet and sticky syrup used in many Lebanese desserts is made from sugar, water, and lemon juice.
4. The most common ingredients in Lebanese desserts include honey, pistachios, and almonds.
5. In Lebanese culture, serving sweet treats at the end of a meal is a symbol of hospitality and generosity.
6. "Ashta" is a type of clotted cream that is used in many traditional Lebanese desserts, including "Mahaleb."
7. "Atayef" are sweet, stuffed pancakes that are often filled with nut or cream filling.
8. "Znoud el Sit" is a sweet, rolled pastry that is filled with nuts and topped with syrup.
9. "Namoura" is a popular semolina cake that is flavored with anise, cinnamon, and orange blossom water.
10. In Lebanon, dessert is often accompanied by a cup of strong Arabic coffee, which is believed to aid in digestion.

Qatayef

Qatayef is a traditional Lebanese dessert that is typically served during the holy month of Ramadan. This sweet, stuffed pancake is made from a batter of flour, yeast, and sugar and is filled with a variety of sweet fillings, including cheese, nuts, and sweet syrup. Qatayef is then fried to perfection, creating a crispy exterior and a soft, gooey interior.

 4 SERVINGS   90 MINUTES   400 KCAL    MED

INGREDIENTS

- 1 cup all-purpose flour
- 1 tsp active dry yeast
- 1 tbsp sugar
- 1/4 tsp salt
- 1/2 cup warm water
- 1 cup ricotta cheese
- 1/2 cup chopped walnuts
- 1 tbsp orange blossom water
- 2 cups of syrup (1 cup sugar and 1 cup of water)
- Vegetable oil, for frying

DIRECTIONS

1. In a medium bowl, combine the flour, yeast, sugar, and salt.
2. Gradually add the warm water while stirring, until the mixture forms a smooth batter.
3. Cover the bowl with a damp cloth and let the batter rise in a warm place for 45 minutes.
4. In a separate bowl, mix the ricotta cheese, walnuts, and orange blossom water.
5. Preheat 2-3 inches of vegetable oil in a deep saucepan over medium heat.
6. Scoop a small amount of batter into the palm of your hand, creating a small indentation in the center.
7. Fill the indentation with a teaspoon of the cheese and nut mixture.
8. Fold the edges of the batter over the filling, sealing the edges to form a ball shape.
9. Fry the Qatayef in the hot oil until they are golden brown, about 3 minutes.
10. Remove the Qatayef from the oil and place on a paper towel to drain excess oil.
11. In a separate saucepan, make the syrup by combining sugar and water and bring to a boil.
12. Once the syrup has thickened, remove from heat and let cool.
13. Serve the Qatayef warm, drizzled with the syrup.

Znoud El Sit

Znoud El Sit is a traditional Lebanese dessert that consists of phyllo dough stuffed with a sweet mixture of nuts, sugar, and cinnamon. This dish is often served during special occasions such as weddings and holidays and is a staple in Lebanese cuisine.

 8 SERVINGS 30 MINUTES  400 KCAL ☆ MED

INGREDIENTS

- 1 package of phyllo dough
- 1 cup of finely chopped mixed nuts (walnuts, almonds, and pistachios)
- 1 cup of granulated sugar
- 1 tablespoon of ground cinnamon
- 1/2 cup of melted unsalted butter
- Powdered sugar for dusting

DIRECTIONS

1. Preheat your oven to 350°F (180°C). Line a large baking sheet with parchment paper.
2. In a large bowl, mix together the chopped nuts, sugar, and cinnamon until well combined.
3. Cut the phyllo dough into 2-inch wide strips. Take one strip of phyllo dough and brush it with melted butter. Repeat this process with two more layers of phyllo.
4. Place a spoonful of the nut mixture at the end of the strip and roll it tightly into a cylinder shape. Repeat this process with the remaining phyllo dough and nut mixture.
5. Place the rolls on the prepared baking sheet and brush them with the remaining melted butter. Bake for 25-30 minutes, or until the phyllo is golden brown.
6. Once the Znoud El Sit is finished baking, remove it from the oven and let it cool for a few minutes. Dust it with powdered sugar and serve it warm.

Enjoy the sweet and flaky pastry that is the traditional Lebanese dessert, Znoud El Sit! This dish is sure to be a hit with your family and friends, especially during special occasions.

Ghraybeh

Ghraybeh is a traditional Lebanese sweet that is popular for its delicate, buttery flavor and flaky texture. This sweet is a staple in many Lebanese households, especially during special occasions like weddings and religious holidays. Ghraybeh has been around for centuries and is believed to have originated from the Middle Eastern region.

8 SERVINGS   **45** MINUTES   **200** KCAL   EASY

INGREDIENTS

- 1 cup unsalted butter, at room temperature
- 1/2 cup powdered sugar
- 1 teaspoon orange blossom water
- 2 cups all-purpose flour
- Pinch of salt

DIRECTIONS

1. In a large mixing bowl, cream together the butter and powdered sugar until smooth and creamy.
2. Stir in the orange blossom water.
3. In a separate bowl, whisk together the flour and salt.
4. Gradually add the flour mixture to the butter mixture, mixing until just combined.
5. Knead the dough briefly on a lightly floured surface until it comes together.
6. Shape the dough into a ball and wrap it in plastic wrap. Chill for at least 30 minutes.
7. Preheat the oven to 350°F. Line a baking sheet with parchment paper.
8. Roll the chilled dough into small balls, about the size of a walnut.
9. Place the balls on the prepared baking sheet, spacing them about 2 inches apart.
10. Use a fork to gently press down on each ball, making a crisscross pattern.
11. Bake for 15-20 minutes, or until the edges are lightly golden.
12. Remove from the oven and let cool completely on the baking sheet.
13. Serve with tea or coffee.

Layali Lubnan

Layali Lubnan is a traditional Lebanese dessert that is made with vermicelli pasta, sugar, and milk. It is a sweet, creamy pudding that is flavored with cinnamon and vanilla and is often garnished with chopped nuts. This dish has a rich history in Lebanese cuisine and is typically served at special occasions and celebrations.

6 SERVINGS   **60** MINUTES   **400** KCAL   EASY

INGREDIENTS

- 1 cup vermicelli pasta, broken into small pieces
- 1 cup granulated sugar
- 1 cup whole milk
- 1 cup heavy cream
- 2 teaspoons cinnamon
- 1 teaspoon vanilla extract
- 1/4 teaspoon salt
- 1/4 cup chopped almonds or pistachios, for garnish

DIRECTIONS

1. In a large saucepan, cook the vermicelli pasta over medium heat until golden brown, stirring occasionally.
2. Remove from heat and set aside.
3. In the same saucepan, combine the sugar, milk, heavy cream, cinnamon, vanilla extract, and salt.
4. Cook over medium heat, stirring continuously, until the sugar has dissolved.
5. Stir in the cooked vermicelli pasta.
6. Continue cooking, stirring occasionally, until the pudding thickens, about 15-20 minutes.
7. Remove from heat and let cool.
8. Pour the pudding into serving dishes.
9. Garnish with chopped almonds or pistachios.
10. Serve chilled or at room temperature.

Cheese knafeh

A sweet, cheesy, and crunchy dessert, Cheese Knafeh is a traditional Middle Eastern treat that is believed to have originated in the Palestinian city of Nablus. Made with shredded phyllo dough, melted cheese, and sweet syrup, this dish is a favorite in countries such as Lebanon, Jordan, and Syria.

 6 SERVINGS    **60** MINUTES   **500** KCAL    MED

INGREDIENTS

- 1 pound shredded phyllo dough
- 1 pound creamy cheese (such as Nabulsi or Akkawi cheese)
- 1 cup unsalted butter, melted
- 1 cup simple syrup
- 1 teaspoon orange blossom water (optional)
- 1/2 cup chopped pistachios, for garnish

DIRECTIONS

1. Preheat oven to 350°F.
2. In a large bowl, mix the shredded phyllo dough with melted butter and set aside.
3. In a 9x13 inch baking dish, spread half of the phyllo mixture evenly on the bottom of the dish.
4. Sprinkle the cheese on top of the phyllo mixture.
5. Cover the cheese with the remaining phyllo mixture, pressing down gently to ensure the cheese is fully covered.
6. Bake in the oven for 30-35 minutes, or until the top is golden brown.
7. While the knafeh is baking, prepare the simple syrup by heating 1 cup of sugar and 1 cup of water in a saucepan over medium heat. Stir until the sugar has dissolved, then add orange blossom water (if using).
8. Once the knafeh is done baking, remove from the oven and immediately pour the simple syrup over the top.
9. Sprinkle chopped pistachios over the knafeh and allow it to cool for 10 minutes.
10. Serve warm and enjoy the sweet, cheesy, crunchy goodness!

Honey Ashta

Honey Ashta is a traditional Lebanese dessert that combines the rich, creamy texture of Ashta (a type of clotted cream) with the sweetness of honey. This dessert has a long history in Lebanese cuisine and is often served during special occasions such as weddings and religious holidays.

  6 SERVINGS **30** MINUTES **400** KCAL  EASY

INGREDIENTS

- 2 cups Ashta cream
- 1/2 cup honey
- 1 teaspoon orange blossom water (optional)
- 1/2 cup chopped pistachios, for garnish
- 30 sheets of phyllo dough (optional)

DIRECTIONS

1. In a large bowl, mix the Ashta cream with honey until fully combined.
2. Stir in the orange blossom water (if using).
3. If using phyllo dough, preheat oven to 375°F.
4. Cut the phyllo dough into small squares and place a spoonful of the Ashta mixture in the center of each square.
5. Fold the edges of the phyllo dough up around the Ashta mixture to form a small package.
6. Place the packages on a baking sheet and bake in the oven for 10-12 minutes, or until the phyllo is golden brown.
7. If not using phyllo dough, simply place the Ashta mixture in individual serving dishes.
8. Sprinkle chopped pistachios over the Ashta and allow to cool for 10 minutes.
9. Serve and enjoy the sweet, creamy taste of traditional Lebanese Ashta!

CHAPTER 7

Drinks

Lebanese drinks are a vibrant and diverse part of the country's rich culinary heritage. From sweet and refreshing juices to warm and comforting coffee, Lebanese drinks offer something for everyone. These drinks are not just a simple thirst quencher, they are a reflection of the country's rich history, culture, and traditions.

Lebanon has a long history of hospitality and the art of making and enjoying drinks is an integral part of this tradition. From the traditional mint tea served in the countryside to the freshly squeezed orange juice enjoyed at the local cafes, Lebanese drinks are a staple in every household.

The country's location at the crossroads of Europe, Asia, and Africa has greatly influenced its cuisine and drinks. The climate in Lebanon is perfect for growing a wide variety of fruits, herbs, and spices, and these ingredients are used to create unique and delicious drinks. Whether you are a fan of sweet and fruity drinks or prefer something with a bit more kick, you will find something to suit your taste in Lebanese cuisine.

One of the most popular drinks in Lebanon is Arak, a traditional spirit made from aniseed. Arak is often enjoyed as an aperitif before a meal or served with mezze, a selection of small dishes that is a staple of Lebanese cuisine. Another popular drink is Jallab, a sweet syrup made from dates, raisins, and grape molasses, which is often served over ice and sprinkled with pine nuts.

Lebanese coffee is also a staple in the country and is enjoyed at any time of the day. The coffee is brewed using Arabic coffee pots and is served in small cups, often accompanied by sweets. Freshly squeezed juices are also a popular drink, with lemon and mint being a particularly popular combination.

In this Lebanese Recipes book, we will explore the world of Lebanese drinks and show you how to create some of the country's most popular and delicious drinks in your own home. Whether you are looking for a refreshing and sweet juice or a warm and comforting coffee, you will find the perfect recipe in these pages. So why not explore the rich and diverse world of Lebanese drinks today and discover a new favorite drink.

Did you know that...

1. Arak is the national drink of Lebanon and is made from aniseed, which gives it its unique flavor.
2. Jallab, a sweet syrup made from dates, raisins, and grape molasses, is a popular drink in Lebanon and is often served over ice.
3. Lebanese coffee is brewed using traditional Arabic coffee pots and is served in small cups, often accompanied by sweets.
4. Freshly squeezed juices are a staple in Lebanon, and lemon and mint is a particularly popular combination.
5. Tea is a popular drink in Lebanon, and mint tea is a traditional drink often served during Ramadan.
6. The traditional spirit Arak is often enjoyed as an aperitif before a meal or served with mezze, a selection of small dishes that is a staple of Lebanese cuisine.
7. Jallab syrup is often mixed with water and rose water to create a sweet and refreshing drink.
8. Lebanese coffee is traditionally brewed with cardamom, which gives it a unique and fragrant flavor.
9. Lebanese drinks often use ingredients such as pomegranate juice, rose water, and orange blossom water, which are native to the region.
10. The practice of serving drinks with sweets is an important part of Lebanese hospitality and is a symbol of welcoming guests into the home.

Sahlab

Sahlab is a warm and comforting drink that is popular in Lebanon and other Middle Eastern countries. Made from a mixture of hot milk, spices, and sugar, this drink is perfect for cold winter nights or as a comforting dessert. The recipe for Sahlab has been passed down for generations, and each family has their own unique twist on the traditional recipe.

 4 SERVINGS   10 MINUTES   150 KCAL   EASY

INGREDIENTS

- 4 cups of whole milk
- 2 tablespoons of cornstarch
- 2 tablespoons of sugar
- 1 teaspoon of cinnamon
- 1 teaspoon of vanilla extract
- A pinch of salt
- Optional: sliced almonds, raisins, or coconut flakes for garnish

DIRECTIONS

1. In a saucepan, mix together the cornstarch and 1/2 cup of the milk until the cornstarch is fully dissolved.
2. Add the remaining milk, sugar, cinnamon, vanilla extract, and salt to the saucepan and stir to combine.
3. Place the saucepan over medium heat and cook, stirring constantly, until the mixture begins to thicken, about 5 minutes.
4. Reduce the heat to low and continue to cook for an additional 2-3 minutes, stirring constantly, until the mixture is thick and creamy.
5. Pour the Sahlab into serving glasses and garnish with sliced almonds, raisins, or coconut flakes if desired.
6. Serve the Sahlab hot and enjoy the comforting and warm flavors of this traditional Middle Eastern drink.

Sahlab is a simple and delicious drink that is perfect for cozy nights in or as a comforting dessert. Whether you prefer it sweet or with a little less sugar, this recipe is easily customizable to suit your taste. So why not try making Sahlab today and discover the comforting and warm flavors of this traditional Middle Eastern drink.

Assir Limoun

Sweet Lime Drink, also known as Assir Limoun, is a traditional Lebanese drink that is both refreshing and thirst-quenching. Made with fresh lime juice, sugar, and water, this simple yet delicious drink is a staple in Lebanese households, especially during the hot summer months. The sweet and tart flavors of this drink make it the perfect refreshment on a hot day.

4 SERVINGS   **10** MINUTES   **50** KCAL   EASY

INGREDIENTS

- 4 large limes, juiced
- 1/2 cup of sugar
- 4 cups of water
- Optional: ice and mint leaves for garnish

DIRECTIONS

1. In a small saucepan, combine the sugar and 1/2 cup of water. Cook over medium heat, stirring constantly, until the sugar is fully dissolved, about 2-3 minutes.
2. Remove the saucepan from heat and let it cool for 5 minutes.
3. In a pitcher, combine the lime juice, sugar syrup, and remaining water. Stir to combine.
4. Taste the mixture and adjust the sweetness to your liking by adding more sugar syrup if necessary.
5. Pour the Sweet Lime Drink into glasses filled with ice and garnish with mint leaves if desired.
6. Serve the Sweet Lime Drink immediately and enjoy the refreshing and thirst-quenching flavors of this traditional Lebanese drink.

Sweet Lime Drink is a staple in Lebanese households and is the perfect refreshment on a hot summer day. Whether you enjoy it plain or with a touch of mint, this simple and delicious drink is sure to quench your thirst and cool you down. So why not try making Sweet Lime Drink today and discover the refreshing and thirst-quenching flavors of this traditional Lebanese drink.

Ma Zahar

Orange Blossom Water, also known as Ma Zahar, is a traditional Lebanese drink that is often used in Lebanese sweets and desserts. Made from the distillation of orange blossom petals, this fragrant water adds a delicate and floral flavor to any dish. In addition to its use in cooking and baking, Orange Blossom Water is also enjoyed as a standalone drink and is often mixed with water or lemon juice for a refreshing and hydrating beverage.

 4 SERVINGS   5 MINUTES   10 KCAL   EASY

INGREDIENTS

- 1/2 cup Orange Blossom Water
- 4 cups water
- 1 orange juice
- Ice
- Optional: sugar to taste

DIRECTIONS

1. In a pitcher, combine the Orange Blossom Water, water, and lemon juice (if using).
2. Stir to combine.
3. If desired, add sugar to taste.
4. Taste the mixture and adjust the sweetness to your liking by adding more sugar if necessary.
5. Add ice to the pitcher and stir.
6. Add orange juice
7. Pour the Orange Blossom Water into glasses.
8. Serve the Orange Blossom Water immediately and enjoy the refreshing and fragrant combination of water, lemon juice, and Orange Blossom Water.

Orange Blossom Water is a versatile and fragrant ingredient that can be used in many different ways. Whether you enjoy it as a standalone drink or use it in baking and cooking, Orange Blossom Water is sure to add a delicate and floral flavor to any dish. So why not try making Orange Blossom Water today and discover the refreshing and hydrating qualities of this traditional Lebanese drink.

Sharab Al-inek

Grape Syrup Drink, also known as Sharab Al-inek, is a traditional Lebanese beverage that is made from freshly pressed grape juice and sugar. This sweet and flavorful drink is a staple in Lebanese households and is often enjoyed as a refreshing treat during the warm summer months. In addition to its delicious taste, Grape Syrup Drink is also known for its hydrating properties and is often used to help rehydrate the body after a long day in the sun.

4 SERVINGS   **5** MINUTES   **140** KCAL   EASY

INGREDIENTS

- 4 cups fresh grape juice
- 2 cups sugar
- 1 cup water
- Ice
- Optional: lemon juice to taste

DIRECTIONS

1. In a saucepan, combine the grape juice, sugar, and water.
2. Stir the mixture until the sugar is dissolved.
3. Bring the mixture to a boil over medium heat.
4. Reduce the heat and let the mixture simmer for 5-10 minutes.
5. Remove the saucepan from heat and let the mixture cool completely.
6. Once cooled, pour the Grape Syrup Drink into a pitcher.
7. Add ice to the pitcher and stir.
8. If desired, add lemon juice to taste.
9. Taste the mixture and adjust the sweetness to your liking by adding more sugar if necessary.
10. Pour the Grape Syrup Drink into glasses.
11. Serve the Grape Syrup Drink immediately and enjoy the sweet and refreshing taste of this traditional Lebanese beverage.
12. Grape Syrup Drink is a delicious and hydrating beverage that is perfect for any time of year. Whether you are looking for a sweet treat to enjoy during the hot summer months or simply want to hydrate after a long day, Grape Syrup Drink is the perfect drink for you. So why not try making Grape Syrup Drink today and discover the delicious and refreshing taste of this traditional Lebanese beverage.

Shai Baida

Lebanese Iced Tea, also known as Shai Baida, is a traditional Lebanese drink that is both refreshing and flavorful. Made with black tea, sugar, and a hint of lemon, this simple yet delicious drink is a staple in Lebanese households and is often served as a refreshment on a hot day. The sweet and tangy flavors of this drink make it the perfect accompaniment to any meal or as a refreshing break in between.

 4 SERVINGS    10 MINUTES   50 KCAL   EASY

INGREDIENTS

- 4 black tea bags
- 1/2 cup of sugar
- 4 cups of water
- 1 lemon, juiced
- Ice
- Optional: mint leaves for garnish

DIRECTIONS

1. In a medium saucepan, bring the water to a boil.
2. Once the water is boiling, remove the saucepan from heat and add the tea bags.
3. Let the tea steep for 5 minutes.
4. In a small saucepan, combine the sugar and 1/2 cup of water. Cook over medium heat, stirring constantly, until the sugar is fully dissolved, about 2-3 minutes.
5. Remove the saucepan from heat and let it cool for 5 minutes.
6. Remove the tea bags from the tea and let it cool to room temperature.
7. In a pitcher, combine the tea, sugar syrup, lemon juice, and ice. Stir to combine.
8. Taste the mixture and adjust the sweetness to your liking by adding more sugar syrup if necessary.
9. Pour the Lebanese Iced Tea into glasses and garnish with mint leaves if desired.
10. Serve the Lebanese Iced Tea immediately and enjoy the refreshing and flavorful combination of tea, sugar, lemon, and ice.

Lebanese Iced Tea is the perfect drink to enjoy on a hot day. Whether you enjoy it plain or with a touch of mint, this simple and delicious drink is sure to refresh and quench your thirst. So why not try making Lebanese Iced Tea today and discover the sweet and tangy flavors of this traditional Lebanese drink.

CONCLUSIONS

Lebanese cuisine is a true celebration of life and culture, and the recipes in this book are a testament to the rich culinary heritage of Lebanon. From the mezze platters to the main dishes, from the sweets to the drinks, each recipe is a unique expression of the country's diverse culinary traditions. From the warm spices used in the dishes, to the bright and zesty flavors of the fresh ingredients, the flavors of Lebanon are like no other in the world.

Throughout this book, you have been introduced to some of the most popular and traditional Lebanese dishes, each with its own unique story and history. Whether you are an experienced cook or just starting out, the recipes in this book are accessible and easy to follow, and will help you bring the flavors of Lebanon into your own kitchen.

The recipes in this book are just a glimpse into the world of Lebanese cuisine, and we hope that they inspire you to explore this rich and diverse cuisine further. From the bold spices used in the dishes, to the sweet and floral flavors of the drinks, the recipes in this book will take you on a culinary journey through the heart of Lebanon.

So, we invite you to gather your friends and family around the table, pour a glass of delicious Lebanese wine, and savor the flavors of this amazing country. Whether you are cooking a traditional meal or experimenting with a new recipe, the memories and flavors of Lebanese cuisine will remain with you for a lifetime. In conclusion, Lebanese cuisine is not just about the food, but it is about the people, the culture, and the way of life. So let's raise a glass of sweet Arak to celebrate the rich culinary traditions of this beautiful country and the memories that are created around the dinner table.